W9-AZV-347

DOGS SET II

Yorkshire Terriers

Stuart A. Kallen
ABDO & Daughters

visit us at
www.abdopub.com

Published by Abdo & Daughters, 4940 Viking Drive, Suite 622, Edina, Minnesota 55435.

Copyright © 1998 by Abdo Consulting Group, Inc., Pentagon Tower, P.O. Box 36036, Minneapolis, Minnesota 55435 USA. International copyrights reserved in all countries. No part of this book may be reproduced in any form without written permission from the publisher.

Printed in the United States.

Cover Photo credits: Peter Arnold, Inc.
Interior Photo credits: Peter Arnold, Inc.

Edited by Bob Italia

Library of Congress Cataloging-in-Publication Data

Kallen, Stuart A., 1955-
       Yorkshire terriers / Stuart A. Kallen.
       p. cm. -- (Dogs. Set II)
       Includes index.
       Summary: Describes the physical characteristics and habits of "Yorkies" and the care they require as a pet.
       ISBN 1-56239-577-7
       1. Yorkshire terriers--Juvenile literature. [1. Yorkshire terriers. 2. Dogs.] I. Title. II. Series: Kallen, Stuart A., 1955-   Dogs Set II.

       SF429.Y6K35   1998
       636.76--dc21
                                                        97-14828
                                                        CIP
                                                        AC

Second printing 2002

Contents

Dogs and Wolves—
Close Cousins

Dogs have been living with humans for more than 12,000 years. Today, millions of dogs live in the world. Over 400 **breeds** exist. And, believe it or not, all dogs are related to the wolf.

Some dogs—like tiny poodles or Great Danes—may look nothing like wolves. But under their skin, every dog shares many feelings and **traits** with wolves.

The dog family is called Canidae, from the Latin word *canis*, meaning "dog." The canid family has 37 **species**. They include foxes, jackals, wild dogs, and wolves.

Opposite page: A Yorkshire terrier standing.

Yorkshire Terriers

Yorkshire terriers are cute little dogs with very long, silky hair. Sometimes they are called "Yorkies." Yorkies are in the class of "Toy" dogs because they are so small and cuddly. Scottish weavers brought the dogs to Yorkshire in northern England in the 19th century. Soon they became popular for their small size and beautiful **coats**.

Yorkies came to America in 1880. Since that time the **breed** has become more popular every year.

Opposite page:
Yorkshire terriers are
often called Yorkies.

What They're Like

Yorkies are dogs that love to sit on laps and be carried around. They even like to ride in bicycle baskets! They are friendly and get along well with other pets. Yorkies are smart and love children. Their excitement and joy can be heard in their bark. Yorkies make brave watchdogs.

Yorkies love to live indoors. They can easily be kept in apartments. But they also love to romp and play outdoors.

Opposite page:
Yorkies are friendly
and fun to play with.

Coat and Color

A Yorkshire terrier's **coat** is long, soft, and shiny. It is perfectly straight. Yorkies need their hair trimmed so it does not drag on the floor. Their hair is parted on the nose, all the way down the back, to the tip of the tail. The long hair on the head is sometimes tied up with bows and ribbons.

Yorkies are blue, black, and tan in color. The hair is dark steel-blue from the back of the head to the tip of the tail. The hair on the head is tan to bright gold. The tan hairs are darker at the root than at the tip. They have medium-large, round brown eyes. They are alert and show intelligence.

Opposite page: Yorkies have very shiny coats.

Size

Yorkies are toy dogs that weigh between 3 and 7 pounds (1.3 to 3 kg). They stand 6 to 10 inches (15 to 25 cm) at the shoulder. The body is compact and short. The tail is **docked** at medium length and has plenty of hair.

Yorkies have a small head that is flat at the top, and not too round. The ears are V-shaped and small.

Opposite page: Yorkies are small dogs with compact bodies.

Care

Yorkies make happy members of any family. They love to sit on laps and be pampered.

Like any dog, a Yorkie needs the same thing a human needs: a warm bed, food, water, exercise, and lots of love.

Yorkies have long hair that needs to be brushed every day and trimmed every few months. Because of their hair, Yorkies need to be bathed often.

All dogs need shots every year. These shots stop diseases such as **distemper** and **hepatitis**.

As a member of your household, your dog expects love and attention. Yorkshire terriers enjoy human contact. They love to be taken for walks where they can run and explore.

Opposite page: Yorkies like human contact.

Feeding

Like all dogs, Yorkies like to eat meat. But Yorkies need a well-balanced diet. Most dog foods—dry or canned—will give the dog proper **nutrition**.

When you buy a puppy find out what it has been eating and continue that diet. A small puppy needs four or five small meals a day. By six months, it will need only two meals a day. By one year, a single evening feeding will be enough.

Yorkshire terriers must be exercised every day so they do not gain weight. Walking, running, and playing together will keep you and your dog happy and healthy. Give your dog a small rubber ball to play with.

Like any animal, Yorkies need fresh water. Keep water next to the dog's food bowl and change it daily.

Like any dog, a Yorkie
needs a proper diet.

Things They Need

A dog needs a quiet place to sleep. A soft dog bed in a quiet corner is the best place for a Yorkie to sleep. Yorkies should live indoors. Their small size and fine **coat** does not allow them to stand cold weather or rain.

Yorkies love to play and explore. A fenced-in yard is the perfect home for the dog. If that is not possible, use a chain on a runner.

In most cities and towns, dogs must be leashed when going for a walk. It will also need a license. A dog license has the owner's name, address, and telephone number on it. If the dog runs away, the owner can be called.

Opposite page: Yorkies like to live indoors.

Puppies

A Yorkshire terrier can have up to five puppies. The dog is **pregnant** for about nine weeks. When she is ready to give birth, she prefers a dark place away from noises. If your dog is pregnant, give her a strong box lined with an old blanket. She will have her puppies there.

Puppies are tiny and helpless when born. They arrive about a half hour apart. The mother licks them to get rid of the birth sacs and to help them start breathing. Their eyes are shut, making them blind for their first nine days. They are also deaf for about ten days.

Dogs are **mammals**. This means they drink milk from their mother. After about four weeks, puppies begin to grow teeth. Separate them from their mother and give the puppies soft dog food.

Your dog
should see a
veterinarian
regularly.

Glossary

breed: a grouping of animals with the same traits.

coat: the dog's outer covering of hair.

distemper: a contagious disease that dogs and other animals get, which is caused by a virus.

dock: the part of an animal's tail after it has been shortened.

hepatitis (hep-uh-TIE-tis): an inflammation of the liver caused by virus.

mammal: a group of animals, including humans, that have hair and feed their young milk.

nutrition (new-TRISH-un): food; nourishment.

pregnant: with one or more babies growing inside the body.

species (SPEE-sees): a kind or type.

trait: a feature of an animal.

veterinarian: a doctor trained to take care of animals.

Internet Sites

Tip Top Yorkshire Terrier Home Page
http://www.mindspring.com/~yorkie/
This site has many links to other terrier sites, it also has an array of photos of terriers, as well as information on taking care of a terrier.

The Yorkshire Terrier Magazine
http://www.armory.com/~terrier/
Published bi-monthly (6 times a year) each issue carefully combines educational and informative articles, reader opinions, beautiful advertisements, and many photos all reproduced with the highest quality printing. Additional features include: show statistics, veterinary information, specialty reports, candid interviews with breeders, breeders forums and more.

These sites are subject to change. Go to your favorite search engine and type in Yorkshire Terrier for more sites.

Index